QUICK JOB INTERVIEW GUIDE

Seven Steps to Acing Your Interview

Michael Farr
with The Editors at JIST

Contents

JIST Works
America's Career Publisher

Quick Job Interview Guide Is Short, But It May Be All You Need

After all, this little book has one ultimate goal: to help you quickly improve your job interview skills. Despite all the advances in hiring technology, most people still get hired—or, more often, screened out—based on a personal interview. Of course, you need the necessary job-related skills to be *considered* for a job, but how well you do in the interview often makes the difference in whether you *get* a job offer or not.

In just seven steps, this book can help you succeed at your next interview and get the job of your dreams. More specifically it can

- Give you techniques to present yourself more effectively in an interview, because just a few hours of learning and practice is often enough to make a big difference.
- Show you how to get more interviews in the first place, follow up after an interview, and negotiate your salary.
- Help you find a good fit by helping you identify the skills you have and then clearly define where and how you want to use them.

The interviewing techniques in this book are based on decades of research and common sense. Many of the methods I suggest have been field tested over many years. My interest has always been to find more effective ways to help people get good jobs in less time.

Trust Me—Do the Worksheets. I know you will resist completing the worksheets in this book. But trust me, they are worth your time. Doing them will give you a better sense of what you are good at, why someone should hire you, and how to answer those tough interview questions that you dread. Once you have finished this book and its activities, you will have spent more time preparing for a job interview than most people.

Why Such a Short Book? I have often been asked to tell someone, in a few minutes or hours, the most important things they should know and do to succeed in a job interview. Instructors and counselors also ask the same question because they only have a short time to spend with the folks they're trying to help. I've given this a lot of thought, and the seven topics in this book are the ones I think are most important to know.

This book is short enough to look over in the morning in order to ace a job interview in the afternoon. Granted, doing all of the activities would take more time, but they will also prepare you far better than scanning the book. Of course there are bigger books out there about job interviews, but *Quick Job Interview Guide* may be all you need.

I wish you well in your interviews and your life.

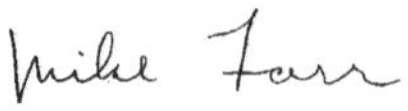

The Seven Steps for Interview Success

The best way to prepare for an interview is to research the organization and the job, get a good handle on your qualifications and experience, and carefully consider your responses to the tough questions that might come up. This book is organized around seven steps that will help you do all of those things and then some.

1. Learn the Basics and Make a Positive Impression
2. Know Who You Are and What You Can Do
3. Do Your Homework and Come Prepared
4. Answer Key Interview Questions with Ease
5. Handle Tough Interview Situations with Confidence
6. Follow Up
7. Negotiate Your Way to a Fair Salary

Take the time to read the information and complete the worksheets for each of the seven steps in this booklet. When you've finished, you'll have the skills and knowledge you need to impress your interviewer and land your next job.

STEP 1: Learn the Basics and Make a Positive Impression

The interview is the most important 60 minutes in the job search. Yet research indicates that most people are not well-prepared for the interview process. This can be good news for you, because reading this book can help you improve your interviewing skills and give you an advantage over the majority of job seekers.

Although the interview itself is an incredibly complex interaction, I have found that there are simple things you can do that make a big difference in getting a job offer. This first step gives you the most essential information you need to know to succeed in your interview.

Eight Keys to Interview Success

Few job seekers have a clear sense of what they need to accomplish in an interview. What follows will help you get a quick understanding of the most important things to do in these critical minutes.

1. Make a Positive Impression

Employers rarely hire someone who makes a negative impression. These tips can help you make a positive one before, during, and after your interview.

Before the Interview

There are three ways an interviewer may form an impression of you before meeting you face-to-face:

- **The interviewer already knows you.** An employer may know you from previous contacts or from someone else's description. In this situation, you should acknowledge that relationship, but treat the interview in all other respects as a business meeting.
- **You have contacted the interviewer through e-mail or by phone.** Both kinds of contact give an impression of your communication skills and ability to present yourself in a competent way. You should also call the day before the interview to verify the time of your meeting and get any directions you need. This is just another way to demonstrate your attention to detail and shows the importance you place on the interview.
- **The interviewer has read your resume and other materials.** Prior to most interviews, you provide the employer with information that creates an impression. Sending a note, letter, or e-mail beforehand often creates the impression that you are well-organized. Applications, resumes, and other correspondence sent or e-mailed in advance help interviewers know more about you and also contribute to their impression of you.

Quip

Receptionists and other staff you have contact with will mention their observations of you to the interviewer, so be professional and courteous at all times.

The Day of the Interview

To make a good impression on interview day, use these tips:

- **Get there on time.** Ask for directions from the receptionist to be sure you know how to get to the interview. Plan on arriving for the interview 5 to 10 minutes early, allowing time for traffic and other problems.

- **Check your appearance.** Arrive early enough to slip into a restroom and check your grooming. You would be surprised how many people go into the interview with wind-blown hair or smudged lipstick on their teeth. Use a breath mint just to be on the safe side, but do not spray on perfume, cologne, or hair spray right before the interview.
- **Use appropriate waiting-room behavior.** Try to relax as you wait for the interview to begin. Occupy yourself with something businesslike. Review your notes on questions you might like to ask or key skills you want to present. The waiting room may have publications from the organization itself that you might want to look through as well.
- **Be prepared if the interviewer is late.** In fact, hope that it happens. If you arrive promptly but have to wait past the appointed time, that puts the interviewer in a "Gee, I'm sorry, I owe you one" frame of mind. If the interviewer is 15 minutes late, approach the office manager or administrative assistant and politely ask when the interviewer will be free. If you have to wait more than 25 minutes beyond the scheduled time, you may want to ask to reschedule the interview. Set up a new time and accept any apology with a smile. When you do come back for your interview, the interviewer should be even more receptive.
- **Be particular about your dress and appearance.** How you dress and groom can create a big impression (negative or positive), but determining the correct approach can be difficult. To avoid the complexity, follow this simple rule: Dress and groom like the interviewer is likely to be dressed and groomed, but just a little better.
- **Give a firm handshake and maintain good eye contact.** If the employer offers his or her hand, give a firm (but not too firm) handshake and smile. Avoid staring, but do look at the interviewer when either of you is speaking. This tells the employer that you are listening closely and have good social skills.
- **Act interested and alert.** When you are sitting, lean slightly forward in your chair and keep your head up, looking directly at the interviewer.
- **Eliminate annoying behaviors.** Try to eliminate any distracting movements or mannerisms. Avoid tapping your feet or playing with your hair. Listen to yourself and you may notice that you say "aaahhh" or "ummmmm" frequently or use other repetitive words or phrases that you need to avoid. Ask friends or family for help pinpointing these behaviors.
- **Pay attention to your voice.** If you are naturally soft-spoken, work on speaking louder. Listen to news announcers and other professionals who

are good models for volume, speed, and voice tone. If you have a deep or monotone voice, try to vary your intonation—you don't want to put your interviewer to sleep.

- **Use the interviewer's formal name as often as possible.** Do this particularly in the early part of the interview and again when you are ending it. Do not call the interviewer by his or her first name unless the interviewer asks you to.
- **Play the chitchat game for awhile.** Interviewers often comment on the weather, ask if you had trouble getting there, or make some other common opening. These informal openings are standard measures of your social skills. Be friendly and make a few appropriate comments.

> **Quip**
>
> Comment on something personal in the interviewer's office. "I love your office! Did you decorate it yourself?" or "I noticed the model sailboat. Do you sail?" Expressing interest in something that interests the employer works as a compliment. It also provides an opportunity to share something you have in common, so try to pick a topic you know something about.

- **Ask some opening questions.** When the chitchat is over, be prepared to guide the interview in the direction you wish it to go. The section "Use Control Statements to Your Advantage" will show you how.

2. Communicate Your Skills

Once you have made a positive impression, you are ready to tell the interviewer why she should hire you. This back-and-forth conversation usually lasts from 15 to 45 minutes and many consider it to be the most important and most difficult task in the entire job search. Your goal is to know what skills are required to do well in the job and to convince the employer that you have them. Step 2 will help you recognize and communicate your skills.

3. Use Control Statements to Your Advantage

A *control statement* is a statement that steers the conversation. Although you might think you are at the mercy of the interviewer, you do have some ability to set the direction of the interview.

For example, you might say something direct, such as "I'd like to tell you how I can help your organization." Or you might ask, "Would you mind telling me more about your company?" Your control statement can come at the beginning of the interview or any time in the interview when you feel the focus is shifting away from the points *you* want to make.

4. Answer Problem Questions Well

According to employers polled in Northwestern University's Endicott Report, about 80 percent of all job seekers cannot provide a good answer to one or more problem interview questions. Almost everyone has a problem of some sort, and the employer will try to find yours. Expect this and be prepared to provide answers that will put him at ease. Step 5 gives more guidance on answering such questions.

5. Ask the Interviewer Appropriate Questions

Many interviewers will give you the chance to ask questions. How you respond affects their evaluation of you. Having nothing to ask makes you appear passive or disinterested, so be prepared to ask insightful questions about the organization. Good topics to touch on include questions about the style of management, the organization's competition and future obstacles, and how the organization's goals have changed over time.

> **Quip**
>
> Generally, asking about pay, benefits, or other similar topics at this time is unwise. Doing so makes you seem more interested in what the organization can do for *you*, rather than in what you can do for *it*.

6. Tell Employers Why They Should Hire You

Even if the interviewer never directly asks it, she ultimately wants to know one thing: "Why should I hire you over someone else?" A good response to this question usually provides proof that you can help an employer make more money by reducing costs, increasing sales, or solving problems. Step 4 will help you answer this all-important question.

7. Close the Interview Properly

As the interview comes to an end, remember these few things:

- **Don't let the interview last too long.** Most interviews last 30 to 60 minutes. Unless the interviewer asks otherwise, plan on staying no longer than an hour.
- **If a problem came up, repeat your resolution of it.** Whatever you think that particular interviewer may see as a reason not to hire you, bring it up again and present your reasons why you don't see it as a problem.
- **Review your strengths for this job.** Take this opportunity to briefly restate the key skills you possess that relate to this particular job.
- **If you want the job, ask for it.** Employers are more willing to hire someone who is excited about the job.

The Call-Back Close

This interview-closing approach requires some courage, but it does work. Practice it a few times and use it in your early interviews to get more comfortable with it.

1. **Thank the interviewer by name.** Don't forget to smile and shake his hand.
2. **Express interest.** Saying, "I am definitely interested in this position" shows your enthusiasm.
3. **Mention your busy schedule.** It helps to appear active and industrious.
4. **Arrange a reason and a time to call back.** Your goal is to leave a reason for you to get back in touch and to arrange for a specific day and time to do so. For example, say, "I'm sure I'll have questions. When would be the best time for me to get back with you?" Asking "When" does not easily allow a "no" response. Get a specific day and a best time to call.
5. **Say good-bye.**

8. Follow Up After the Interview

Just because the actual interview ended doesn't mean you're done. Following up can make the difference between being unemployed or underemployed and getting the job you want fast. See Step 6 for more details on effective follow-up strategies.

The Three-Step Process for Answering Most Interview Questions

There are thousands of questions that you could be asked in an interview, and there is no way you can memorize a "correct" response for each one. Because interviews are conversational and unpredictable, developing an *approach* to answering an interview question is far more important than memorizing a canned response. The following Three-Step Process can help you fashion an effective answer to most interview questions:

1. **Understand what is really being asked.** Most questions relate to your adaptive skills and personality, i.e. are you dependable, a good worker, or easy to get along with. Other questions really ask whether you have the experience and training to do the job.
2. **Answer the question briefly in a non-damaging way.** A good response to a question should acknowledge the facts of your situation and present them as an advantage rather than a disadvantage.

3. **Answer the real question by presenting your related skills.** An effective response to any interview question should answer by presenting your ability to do the job well.

The following example shows the Three-Step Process at work:

> **Question:** "We were looking for someone with more experience in this field than you seem to have. Why should we consider you over others with better credentials?"

Step 1: Understand What Is Really Being Asked

This question is often asked in a less direct way, but it is a frequent concern of employers. Just remember that employers often hire people who present themselves well in an interview over those with better credentials. Your best shot is to emphasize whatever personal strengths you have that can help you compete with a more experienced worker—for example, that you are a hard worker, that you learn quickly, or that you have skills from other activities that can transfer to this job.

Step 2: Answer the Question Briefly in a Non-damaging Way

The following response answers the question without hurting the person's chances of getting the job:

> "I'm sure there are people who have more years of experience or better credentials. I do, however, have four years of combined training and hands-on experience using the latest methods and techniques. Because my training is recent, I am open to new ideas and am used to working hard and learning quickly."

Step 3: Answer the Real Question by Presenting Your Related Skills

You now have an opportunity to provide additional details that emphasize key skills needed for the job:

> "I held down a full-time job and family responsibilities while going to school. I had an excellent attendance record both at work and school, missing only one day in two years. I also received two merit increases in salary, and my grades were in the top 25 percent of my class. In order to do all this, I had to learn to organize my time and set priorities. With my education complete, I can now turn my full attention to this job. I am willing to work harder than the next person because I have the desire to keep learning and to do an outstanding job."

As in this response, the key is to give examples where you have used the required skills in other settings. Step 4 shows you how to use the Three-Step Process to provide thorough answers to 10 of the most frequently asked questions.

The Prove-It Technique

Most interview questions are an attempt to discover underlying information. You can provide that information in an effective way by using the four-step Prove-It Technique:

1. **Present a concrete example.** People relate to and remember stories. Saying you have a skill is not nearly as powerful as describing a situation where you used that skill.
2. **Quantify.** Whenever possible, use numbers to provide a basis for what you did. For example, give the number of customers served, the percent you exceeded quotas, or the number of new accounts you generated.
3. **Emphasize results.** Providing some data regarding the positive results you obtained is important. For example, stating that profits went up 50 percent.
4. **Link it up.** Although the connection between your example and doing this job well may seem obvious to you, make sure it is clear to the employer.

The next step will help you identify your skills and give you the proof you need to convince an employer to hire you.

STEP 2: Know Who You Are and What You Can Do

According to one survey of employers, more than 90 percent of the people they interview cannot adequately define the skills they have that support their ability to do the job. This step is designed to help you beat that statistic.

Knowing what you are good at is an essential part of doing well in a job interview. Likewise, unless you use the skills that you enjoy using and are good at, you are unlikely to be satisfied in your job.

Quip

Be sure that your top skills are also reflected in your resume. Skills statements on a resume give employers a sense of what you have to offer their organization.

The Three Types of Skills

We all have hundreds of skills, but some will be more important to an employer than others. To help identify your skills, it can be useful to think of them in three major categories: adaptive skills, transferable skills, and job-related skills. The following worksheets and activities will help you identify your key skills. In addition to helping you interview for jobs that you will do well in, being able to communicate your skills can help you write resumes and conduct your job search.

The Skills Employers Want

This information comes from a study conducted jointly by the U.S. Department of Labor and the American Association of Counseling and Development. The study found that most of the skills employers want are either adaptive or transferable skills. Here are the top skills employers identified:

1. Learning to learn
2. Basic academic skills in reading, writing, and computation
3. Good communication skills, including listening and speaking
4. Creative thinking and problem solving
5. Self-esteem, motivation, and goal setting
6. Personal and career development skills
7. Interpersonal/negotiation skills and teamwork
8. Organizational effectiveness and leadership

Always look for opportunities to develop and use these so-called soft skills in your work or to present them clearly in your next interview. Also let the employer know that you are not afraid of learning new skills and that you are confident in your abilities.

Identify Your Adaptive Skills

Adaptive skills are the skills you use every day to survive and function. Some of them could even be considered part of your basic personality. Such skills, which are highly valued by employers, include getting to work on time, honesty, enthusiasm, and getting along with others. To start identifying these skills, answer the question in the box.

What Makes You a Good Worker?

On the following lines, list three things about yourself that you think make you a good worker.

1. ______________________________

2. ______________________________

3. ______________________________

You just listed the most important things for an employer to know about you. Presenting such skills well in an interview will help a less-experienced job seeker get the job over someone with better credentials.

Look over the Adaptive Skills Checklist that follows and check any adaptive skill that you have. You might even circle those skills that you think are most important or feel are your greatest strengths.

Adaptive Skills Checklist

Key Adaptive Skills (those that employers value most)

- ❑ Have good attendance
- ❑ Am honest
- ❑ Arrive on time
- ❑ Follow instructions
- ❑ Meet deadlines
- ❑ Get along with supervisor
- ❑ Get along with coworkers
- ❑ Am hardworking, productive

Other Adaptive Skills

- ❑ Coordinating
- ❑ Results-oriented
- ❑ Mentoring
- ❑ Friendly
- ❑ Ambitious
- ❑ Good-natured
- ❑ Assertive
- ❑ Helpful
- ❑ Capable
- ❑ Intuitive
- ❑ Decisive
- ❑ Culturally tolerant
- ❑ Discreet
- ❑ Quick-learning
- ❑ Eager
- ❑ Loyal
- ❑ Efficient
- ❑ Mature
- ❑ Problem-solving
- ❑ Team player
- ❑ Multitasking
- ❑ Patient
- ❑ Spontaneous
- ❑ Persistent
- ❑ Steady
- ❑ Physically strong
- ❑ Tactful

Other Adaptive Skills (continued)

- ❑ Humble
- ❑ Cheerful
- ❑ Imaginative
- ❑ Modest
- ❑ Expressive
- ❑ Motivated
- ❑ Flexible
- ❑ Responsible
- ❑ Trustworthy
- ❑ Self-confident
- ❑ Versatile
- ❑ Energetic
- ❑ Methodical
- ❑ Enthusiastic
- ❑ Reliable
- ❑ Tenacious
- ❑ Resourceful
- ❑ Thrifty
- ❑ Conscientious
- ❑ Humorous
- ❑ Creative
- ❑ Intelligent
- ❑ Practical
- ❑ Dedicated
- ❑ Competent
- ❑ Independent
- ❑ Well-organized
- ❑ Industrious
- ❑ Original
- ❑ Dependable
- ❑ Open-minded
- ❑ Optimistic
- ❑ Sincere

List any adaptive skills that were not listed but that you think are important to include:

____

____

Now review the checklist and write down the three adaptive skills you feel are *most* important for you to emphasize in an interview.

YOUR TOP ADAPTIVE SKILLS

1. ____
2. ____
3. ____

Identify Your Transferable Skills

Transferable skills are general skills that can be useful in a wide variety of jobs, such as the ability to write clearly or to prioritize tasks. Look over the Transferable Skills Checklist that follows and check any transferable skill that you have. You might even circle those skills that you think are most important or feel are your greatest strengths.

Transferable Skills Checklist

Key Transferable Skills (those that employers value most)

- ❑ Meeting deadlines
- ❑ Managing money or budgets
- ❑ Speaking in public
- ❑ Meeting the public
- ❑ Writing well
- ❑ Solving problems
- ❑ Organizing/managing projects
- ❑ Managing people
- ❑ Negotiating
- ❑ Using computers

Skills Working with Things

- ❑ Driving or operating vehicles
- ❑ Constructing or repairing things
- ❑ Assembling or building things
- ❑ Operating tools/machines

Skills Dealing with Data

- ❑ Analyzing data
- ❑ Investigating
- ❑ Auditing/checking for accuracy
- ❑ Keeping financial records
- ❑ Budgeting
- ❑ Calculating/computing
- ❑ Classifying data
- ❑ Observing/inspecting
- ❑ Comparing/evaluating
- ❑ Counting/taking inventory
- ❑ Research/locating information
- ❑ Paying attention to details
- ❑ Compiling/recording facts
- ❑ Synthesizing

Skills Working with People

- ❑ Administering
- ❑ Instructing others
- ❑ Being diplomatic
- ❑ Demonstrating
- ❑ Being kind
- ❑ Having insight
- ❑ Being outgoing
- ❑ Helping others
- ❑ Being patient
- ❑ Counseling people
- ❑ Being pleasant
- ❑ Interviewing people
- ❑ Being sensitive
- ❑ Listening
- ❑ Being sociable
- ❑ Persuading
- ❑ Being tactful
- ❑ Supervising
- ❑ Being tough
- ❑ Tolerating
- ❑ Caring for others
- ❑ Trusting
- ❑ Coaching
- ❑ Understanding

Skills Working with Words and Ideas

- ❑ Being articulate
- ❑ Designing
- ❑ Speaking publicly
- ❑ Remembering information
- ❑ Writing clearly
- ❑ Corresponding with others
- ❑ Being inventive
- ❑ Communicating verbally
- ❑ Editing
- ❑ Being logical

Leadership Skills

- ❑ Organizing projects
- ❑ Motivating people
- ❑ Being competitive
- ❑ Negotiating agreements
- ❑ Making decisions
- ❑ Planning events
- ❑ Delegating
- ❑ Running meetings
- ❑ Directing others
- ❑ Having self-confidence
- ❑ Explaining to others
- ❑ Motivating yourself
- ❑ Getting results
- ❑ Solving problems
- ❑ Mediating problems
- ❑ Taking risks

Creative or Artistic Skills

- ❑ Being artistic
- ❑ Expressing yourself
- ❑ Drawing
- ❑ Presenting artistic ideas
- ❑ Performing/acting
- ❑ Appreciating music
- ❑ Dancing
- ❑ Playing instruments

Other Similar Transferable Skills You Have

Add any transferable skills that were not listed but that you think are important to include:

____

____

Now review the checklist and write down the five transferable skills you feel are *most* important for you to emphasize in an interview.

Your Top Transferable Skills

1. ______________________________
2. ______________________________
3. ______________________________
4. ______________________________
5. ______________________________

Identify Your Job-Related Skills

Most *job-related skills* are specific to an occupation. An airline pilot obviously needs to know how to fly an airplane (being energetic or articulate isn't enough to stay airborne). Job-related skills are most often gained through work experience, education and training, and hobbies.

The worksheets that follow will help you uncover your job-related skills and accomplishments. When possible, quantify your activities or their results with numbers. Use extra sheets as needed.

Key Accomplishments

List three accomplishments that best prove your ability to do the kind of job you want.

1. ______________________________
2. ______________________________
3. ______________________________

Education and Training Worksheet

Review all your education and training experiences, even those that may have occurred years ago. Some courses may seem more important to certain careers than others. But keep in mind that even the courses that don't seem to support a particular career choice can be an important source of skills. Be sure to emphasize those things that directly support your ability to do the job.

Name of high school(s) and specific years attended

____

Subjects related to job objective

____

____

Related extracurricular activities/hobbies/leisure activities

____

____

Accomplishments/things you did well (in or out of school)

____

____

Schools you attended after high school, specific years attended, and degrees/certificates earned

____

____

Courses related to job objective

____

____

Related extracurricular activities/hobbies/leisure activities

____

____

Accomplishments/things you did well (in or out of school)

____

____

Specific skills you learned that relate to the job you want

____

____

(continued)

(continued)

Other Training

Include formal or informal learning, workshops, military training, skills you learned on the job or from hobbies—anything that will help support your job objective. Include specific dates, certificates earned, or other details as needed.

____

____

____

____

Specific things you learned or can do that relate to the job you want

____

____

Work and Volunteer History Worksheet

List your most recent job first, followed by previous ones. Include military experience, unpaid or volunteer work, and work in a family business as well. If needed, use additional sheets to cover *all* significant paid or unpaid work experiences. Emphasize details and numbers that will help support your accomplishments and prove you have the necessary skills for the job: the number of people served or transactions processed, percentage of sales increase, total budget you were responsible for, etc.

Job 1

Job title(s): ______________________________

Name of organization: ______________________________

Employed from: _______________ to: _______________

How did you help the organization; what did you accomplish and do well? (Be sure to give numbers and details whenever possible.)

____

____

Things you learned; skills you developed or used that relate to the job you want:

____

____

Raises, promotions, positive evaluations, awards:

____

____

Computer software, hardware, and other equipment you used:

____

____

Job 2

Job title(s): ____

Name of organization: ____

Employed from: ____________________ to: ____________________

How did you help the organization; what did you accomplish and do well? (Be sure to give numbers and details whenever possible.)

____

____

Things you learned; skills you developed or used that relate to the job you want:

____

____

Raises, promotions, positive evaluations, awards:

____

____

Computer software, hardware, and other equipment you used:

____

____

(continued)

(continued)

Job 3

Job title(s): ______________________________

Name of organization: ______________________________

Employed from: ______________ to: ______________

How did you help the organization; what did you accomplish and do well? (Be sure to give numbers and details whenever possible.)

____

____

Things you learned; skills you developed or used that relate to the job you want:

____

____

Raises, promotions, positive evaluations, awards:

____

____

Computer software, hardware, and other equipment you used:

____

____

Other Life Experiences Worksheet

Life experiences can be important sources of learning or accomplishment. Think about any hobbies or interests you have had: family responsibilities, recreational activities, travel, or any other experiences in your life where you feel some sense of accomplishment. Write any experiences that seem meaningful to you below and name the key skills you think were involved.

Situation 1:

Describe situation and skills used:

____

Specific things you learned or can do that relate to the job you want:

Situation 2:

Describe situation and skills used:

Specific things you learned or can do that relate to the job you want:

Your Top Job-Related Skills

Of all the job-related skills you have, list the five most important ones you think an employer should know about below:

1. ______
2. ______
3. ______
4. ______
5. ______

Now that you have identified your top skills in all three categories, you are better prepared to answer any question an interviewer throws at you. But there's still more you can do before the actual interview.

STEP 3: Do Your Homework and Come Prepared

You should go to your interview well-prepared to speak about yourself and your accomplishments, but you should have some knowledge about the job, the organization, and the interviewer as well. Gaining that knowledge requires research (otherwise known as work). As a result, many end up treating job information research as they did their high school term papers: They slap it together and hope for the best. This lack of preparation often shows in the interview, which is the reason why the extra work is worth it.

The more you know about the job, the industry, and the employer, the more likely you are to present yourself well in the interview. More importantly, you will be better able to evaluate whether a particular job is right for you.

Research the Industry

Being well-informed about the industry you want to join will help you present yourself well. It can give you a better sense of the growth potential of the organization and the changes that are taking place in the field. The following resources can help you find information about any industry.

Career Guide to Industries

This book, published by the U.S. Department of Labor, provides helpful descriptions for more than 40 major industries, which cover about 75 percent of all jobs. Each description includes an overview of the industry, types of jobs it offers, employment projections, earnings, training required, working conditions, industry trends, and more. You can find the *Career Guide to Industries* in your local library or bookstore or access it online at stats.bls.gov/oco/cg/home.htm. *40 Best Fields for Your Career* (JIST) includes similar information plus useful "best fields" charts for comparing the industries.

Quip

Industry trade magazines such as *Advertising Age, Automotive News, Hotel and Motel Management, Modern Healthcare,* and *Supermarket News* are full of articles detailing trends and issues in their industries. Find the one that covers your industry and read the last few issues.

Hoover's Online

This site (www.hoovers.com) is *the* place to go online to find anything you need to know about industries and employers. You can search for information by company name, industry type, executives' names, and more. Basic information is free.

Encyclopedia of Associations

Found at your library, this resource is a gold mine of associations listed by categories. Each entry gives the contact information, mission statement, newsletters, and conventions for that group. Pick the ones in your industry category that closely match the jobs you are interested in and check out their Web sites.

Research the Careers That Interest You

You probably know what sort of job you want, but learning more about the jobs you're interested in is still a good idea. By researching various options, you can

- **Increase opportunities in your job search by identifying a wider range of job targets.** There are thousands of specialized job titles, and you are almost certain to overlook many that would fit your needs if you don't do some research.
- **Improve your interview skills.** People who do their homework by carefully reading a job description and then mentioning key skills that job requires in an interview often get job offers over those with better credentials.
- **Write a better resume.** Knowing the specific skills a job requires allows you to focus on those skills in your resume and cover letter.

Out of the hundreds of sources of career information, the few that follow will give you most of what you need.

The Occupational Outlook Handbook

The *Occupational Outlook Handbook (OOH)* is the most widely used career information resource available. It provides descriptions for the more than 250 jobs held by nearly 90 percent of the workforce. The *OOH* is updated every two years by the U.S. Department of Labor and provides the latest information on salaries, growth projections, related jobs, required skills, education or training needed, and working conditions. It even indicates trends that are affecting the job and the industry and lists related professional associations and their Web sites.

Quip

Resources such as the *OOH* can help with salary negotiation as well. They can give you a sense of the average salary range for the job you are interested in and even tell you the potential for advancement and promotion.

More specifically, you can use the *OOH* to identify the skills needed in the job you want or to find skills from previous jobs that you can emphasize in an interview. It can also help you discover related jobs that you might have overlooked.

The Occupational Information Network (O*NET)

The U.S. Department of Labor maintains an up-to-date computer database of occupational information. Called the O*NET, it provides detailed information for more than 900 jobs. Although the OOH is more useful for most situations, the O*NET describes many more jobs and provides more details on each one. The complete set of O*NET information is available on the Internet at online.onetcenter.org. A book version published by JIST and titled the *O*NET Dictionary of Occupational Titles* provides the O*NET information of greatest value to most job seekers in an easier-to-use format.

The New Guide for Occupational Exploration

The U.S. Department of Labor has also developed an easy-to-use system that organizes all jobs by interest. This interest-based system is presented in a book titled the *New Guide for Occupational Exploration (GOE)*. The current edition of the *GOE* organizes all jobs into 16 major interest areas. These areas are further divided into more specific work groups of related jobs. The *GOE* allows you to quickly identify groups of jobs that are most closely related to what you want to do and then provides helpful information related to each group.

Research the Company

The best employer information comes from people who work (or used to work) for that organization. These people can often provide you with inside information that can be invaluable in an interview.

If you don't know anyone who works there, then go to the source. Often a receptionist can get you product catalogs, brochures, reports, or other literature that explains the purpose, products, or services of the organization. Studying this information and being able to bring it up during your interview will give you an advantage over most other applicants.

> **Quip**
>
> You may not be able to find much information on small or privately owned companies. In that case, explore comparable companies or pick up the phone and talk with the organization's suppliers, customers, and current employees.

According to librarian Mary-Ellen Mort in Oakland, California, the best sources for information on local organizations are local newspaper articles, local directories, and area trade journals. Some libraries have clipping files of articles on area companies, CEOs, and industries. Ask a reference librarian for assistance.

Online Resources for Company Research

One of the best sources of information on a company can be its own Web site. Search for employer Web sites by using Google or any other search engine. The following resources can also help you research companies:

- **CorporateInformation.com (www.corporateinformation.com):** Type in a company's name to find a brief analysis from this site as well as links to articles and company profiles from other Web sites. Basic registration is free.
- **Google News (news.google.com):** Find the most up-to-date news stories on specific companies, or simply pick the Business section to read current articles. This site is a great way to keep current on industries and specific companies.
- **SuperPages (www.superpages.com):** SuperPages is an enhanced electronic Yellow Pages. Search for U.S. businesses by name and location, or browse by category. Each listing contains contact information as well as a Web site link when available, plus a map and driving directions.
- **Vault (www.vault.com):** This site helps you research companies, industries, and salaries. It also provides job search advice.

Company Research Tutorials

For tips and instructions on researching employers, check out these Web sites:

- **Industry Research Desk (www.virtualpet.com/industry/):** This 19-step process walks you through researching a specific company or a specific industry.
- **Researching Companies Online (www.learnwebskills.com/company/):** This step-by-step tutorial from Internet trainer Debbie Flanagan contains tips for locating free company and industry information on the Web.
- **Riley Guide: Using the Internet to Do Job Search Research (www.rileyguide.com/jsresearch.html):** The first section provides general tips on doing effective Internet research, and the second gives specific advice on finding company information.

Essential Questions Your Research Must Answer

Here are some questions your research should help answer with regards to your interview:

- What is the organization and what does it do?
- What has the organization accomplished in the last three years?
- Where is the organization headed? What new products or services are on the horizon?
- What/who is the competition? Where is this organization at an advantage or disadvantage?
- How can you contribute to the organization's success (provided you get the job)?

Quip

If you're having trouble turning sales slogans into tangible answers, pick up a copy of Leila K. Knight's *Getting the Lowdown on Employers and a Leg Up on the Job Market* (Ten Speed Press) for some down-to-earth, instructive steps in interpreting annual reports.

Research the Job

If you became aware of the job opening through an advertisement, start with the job posting that led you to it. Study it to learn the skills, keywords, and buzzwords it uses. Look up any that are unfamiliar to you.

If you found out about the job through networking and don't have a job posting to refer to, you can request a description of the job from the company. Many companies are required to write detailed descriptions of the job responsibilities and needed skills.

You can also use your network to find someone who works in a similar job. Ask that person what it takes to succeed in the job; then find ways to communicate these qualities to your interviewer.

Research the Interviewer

When it comes to researching your specific interviewer, you may have to resort to the telephone. If you know any of the current employees, politely ask them about this person's style of work, how he or she spends the day, and so forth. The information you dig up could be invaluable (though I don't recommend using any of it as blackmail).

Don't underestimate the power of the Internet either. Go to your favorite search engine (such as Google) and type in the person's name, surrounded by quotation marks. You might find articles about the person's interests and activities, community involvement, or even information related directly to the work he or she does for the company. Use good judgment here, though, because lots of people in the world share the same name.

Ultimately every little bit helps. The more you know about the industry, the company, the job, and the interviewer, the better prepared you will be. Not to mention knowing a lot about a company shows that you are interested in the industry, that you came to the interview prepared, and that you are willing to learn.

STEP 4: Answer Key Interview Questions with Ease

Many employers I've spoken with say that they would have hired someone if that person had just done a bit better in the interview. Spending a little time to learn how to answer the questions covered in this chapter can make an enormous difference to you in getting a job over other qualified applicants.

The 10 Most Frequently Asked Interview Questions—and How to Answer Them

In this section, I use the Three-Step Process from Step 1 to answer the 10 questions you are most likely to be asked in an interview. The sample response that follows each question demonstrates the basic techniques, which you can then apply to your own interview situation.

Question #1: "Why Don't You Tell Me About Yourself?"

It's the classic open-ended interview question. You could start telling your life's history in two hours or less, but that is not what the interviewer wants. Such a question tests your ability to select what is important and communicate it clearly and quickly. Your goal in answering is to relate your background to the position being considered. Try to quickly turn your response to focus on the skills, experience, and training that prepared you for the job.

Sample Answer

A person looking for a managerial position might say something like this:

> "I grew up in the Southwest. My parents both worked and I was active in sports growing up. I always did well in school, and by the time I graduated from high school I had taken a year's worth of

business courses. I knew then that I wanted to work in a business setting. After high school I worked in a variety of jobs and learned a great deal about how various businesses run. For example, I was given complete responsibility for the daily operations of a wholesale distribution company that grossed over two million dollars a year. There I learned to supervise other people and solve problems under pressure. I also became more interested in the financial end of running a business and decided, after three years and three promotions, to seek a position where I could be more involved in key strategies and long-term management decisions."

Such an answer provides a few bits of positive personal history and then quickly turns the interviewer's attention to skills and experiences that directly relate to the job itself.

Honesty Is Always the Best Policy

Almost all career counselors encourage job seekers to be positive about themselves. But they would also caution you to avoid taking credit for something you don't deserve, claiming to have experience you don't have, or bragging excessively about your performance. Just be sure to talk up your achievements, awards, and promotions without misrepresenting yourself.

Question #2: "Why Should I Hire You?"

Though this question is rarely asked so directly, it is the question behind every other question that is asked. It has no hidden meaning, and it is the most important question for you to answer.

So why *should* employers hire you? The best response to this question provides advantages to employers. A good response gives proof that you can help them make more money by improving efficiency, reducing costs, increasing sales, or solving problems (by coming to work on time, improving customer service, managing operations, or bringing a variety of other skills to the job).

Sample Answer

A person with considerable prior experience might offer this response:

"You should hire me because I have a proven track record. I have more than 15 years of education and experience related to this position. More than six of those years have been in management positions similar to this one. In my last position, I was promoted three times in the six years I was there. Most recently I was responsible for supervising a staff of 15 and a warehousing operation that processed over 30 million dollars' worth of materials a year. In the last two years, I managed a 40 percent increase in volume processed with only a 6 percent increase in expenses. I am hardworking and have earned a reputation as a dependable and creative problem solver. I'm eager to apply my experience to new challenges, but I am also willing to ask questions and accept advice from others. This will help me take advantage of what has already been accomplished here."

This response emphasizes the Prove-It Technique from Step 1 by including specific numbers to support each accomplishment. Although the applicant presented her skills and experience in a confident way, she avoided a know-it-all attitude by being open to others' suggestions.

Completing the short worksheet that follows will help you answer this question, though it will be much easier if you have completed the activities in Step 2.

The Reasons Why Someone Should Hire You

List the major advantages you offer an employer in hiring you over someone else. These could be personality traits, transferable skills, special training, prior experience, or anything else you think is important.

1. ______________________________

   ____

2. ______________________________

   ____

3. ______________________________

   ____

Question #3: "What Are Your Major Strengths?"

This question allows you to focus on the credentials you have that will help you succeed on the job. Your response should emphasize your key adaptive or transferable skills, because the decision to hire you is largely based on these skills. You can deal with the details of your specific job-related skills later.

Sample Answer

This response is from a person who has little prior work experience related to the job he now seeks:

> "One of my major strengths is my ability to work hard toward a goal. Once I make a decision to accomplish something, it gets done and done well. For example, I graduated from high school four years ago. At the time I didn't know what I wanted to do, so I looked into joining the Navy. I took the entrance exam and discovered I was much better at understanding complex problems than my grades in high school would suggest. I signed up for a three-year hitch that included intensive training in electronics. I worked hard and graduated in the top 20 percent of my class. I was then assigned to monitor, diagnose, and repair an advanced electronics system that was worth about 20 million dollars. I was promoted several times to the position of Petty Officer and received an honorable discharge after my tour of duty. I now know what I want to do and am prepared to spend extra time learning whatever is needed to do well here."

Quip

Interviewers aren't looking for a life history or an annual report. For the most part you should keep your answers brief and to the point. You can usually elaborate on your skills and experiences throughout the interview, so don't feel like you have to cram it all into one answer.

Remember to provide some proof of your skills, as this response did when citing results of Navy entrance testing and repeated advancement in a highly responsible position.

Question #4: "What Are Your Major Weaknesses?"

You must be prepared to answer this trick question. When I ask this question to groups of job seekers, I usually get two types of responses. The first response goes like this:

> "I really don't have any major weaknesses."

That response is both untrue and evasive. The other type of response I usually get goes something like this:

> "Well, I am really disorganized. I suppose I should do better at that, but my life has just been too hectic, what with the bankruptcy and all."

Although this type of response might get an *A* for honesty, it gets an *F* for interview technique.

What's needed here is an honest, undamaging response followed by something positive to counter the negative. The best approach is to present a weakness in a way that does not harm—and could even help—your ability to do a good job. Here is an example:

Sample Answer

> "I need to learn to be more patient. I often do things myself just because I know I can do them faster and better. This trait sometimes keeps me from delegating tasks effectively. But I am working on it. I'm now spending more time showing others *how* to do the things I want done, and that has helped. They often do better than I expect because I am clear about explaining what I want."

This response could easily be expanded with the Prove-It Technique, but it successfully uses the Three-Step Process to answer this tricky question, presenting the weakness as a positive.

Question #5: "What Sort of Pay Do You Expect to Receive?"

This question is designed to help the employer either eliminate you from consideration or save money at your expense. The employer wants you to name a number that can be compared to a figure the company has in mind. If your figure is too high, you will probably be knocked out of the running. If it's too low, you will make it nearly impossible to negotiate for a higher salary if you *are* offered the job.

Because you aren't likely to get a firm job offer in a first interview, your objective should be to create a positive impression and not be rejected. If the topic of pay does come up, avoid getting nailed down. Here are some things you could say:

> "Are you making me a job offer?" (Corny, yes, but you just might be surprised at the result.)

> "What salary range do you pay for positions with similar requirements?"

> "I'm very interested in the position, and my salary would be negotiable."

> "I prefer to hear more about the position before I can come up with a solid number."

Put off discussion of pay until you are sure it's the real thing and not just part of a screening process. See Step 7 for more information on how to talk money when the time is right.

Question #6: "How Does Your Previous Experience Relate to the Jobs We Have Here?"

This is another direct question that requires a direct response. It requires you to overcome any weaknesses your background might present when you are compared to other job seekers. Here are some typical stumbling blocks:

- You are just out of school and have limited experience in this career.
- This is your first job, or you have not worked for a period of time.
- Your prior work experience is not a match for the tasks required in this job.
- You have had several jobs, but no clear career direction.
- You do not have the education or other credentials many other applicants might have.

Quip

If you have held various short-term jobs, try to emphasize your range of skills and desire for stability. Say something like, "The variety of my experiences is an asset because I have learned so many things I can now apply to this position. Now I am looking for a career where I can settle in, work hard, and move up."

If it is obvious that other job seekers might have more education, more years of experience, or whatever qualifications you lack, acknowledge that, and then counter it with your own strengths.

Sample Answer

"As you know, I have just completed an intensive program in the area of information technology. My educational experience was very thorough, and I have more than 300 hours of interactive computer time as part of my coursework. In addition, I have more than three years of work experience in a variety of business settings, including managing a small business during the absence of the owner. I learned to handle money there and do a variety of basic accounting tasks. I also inventoried and organized products worth over six hundred thousand dollars. These experiences helped me understand the importance of good information technology systems in a business setting. Although I am a recent graduate, my previous business experience allows me to understand how to use what I have learned in practical and effective ways. Because I am new to this career, I plan to work harder and will spend extra time as needed to meet any deadlines."

This response emphasizes transferable skills (knowledge of accounting procedures) and adaptive skills (meeting deadlines and working hard). This emphasis is necessary to counter a lack of previous work experience or job-related skills.

Question #7: "What Are Your Plans for the Future?"

This question explores whether you can be depended on to stay on at this job and work hard. As always, your best approach is an honest one; be prepared to answer the employer's concern in a direct and positive way. Which issues are of concern to an employer depend on the details of your background. For example:

- Will you be happy with the salary? (If not, might you leave?)
- Will you want to have a family? (If so, will you quit or cut your hours to raise children?)
- Do you have a history of leaving jobs after a short period of time? (If so, why won't you leave this one too?)
- Have you just moved to the area or do you appear to be a temporary resident? (If so, you probably won't stay here long either, right?)
- Are you overqualified? (If so, what will keep you from going to a better job as soon as you find one?)

Any of these factors, and many others, can be of concern to an employer. In all cases, try to assure the employer that this is precisely the organization you want to stay with, grow with, and do well with for many years to come.

Sample Answer

This response is from a younger person just entering a new career (the previous position mentioned just happens to be working in a fast food place):

> "I realize I need to establish myself in this field and am eager to get started. I've thought about what I want to do and am sure my skills are the right ones to succeed in this career. For example, I am good at dealing with people. In one position, I provided services to more than 1,000 different people a week. During the 18 months I was there, I served well over 72,000 customers and not once did I get a formal complaint. In fact, I was often complimented on the attention I gave them. There I learned that I enjoy public contact and am delighted at the idea of taking on this position for that reason. I want to learn more about the business and

grow with it. As my value to the organization increases, I hope to be considered for more responsible positions."

The employer wants to know that you will stay on the job and work hard for your pay. This response addresses those concerns.

Question #8: "What Will Your Former Employers (or Teachers, References...) Say About You?"

The interviewer wants to know about your adaptive skills. Are you easy to get along with? Are you a good worker? As you know, many employers check your references before they hire you, so be sure your response matches well with what a former employer or other reference says about you. See Step 5 for more advice on negotiating this problem question.

If you failed in a job, telling the truth is often the best policy. Tell it like it was, but *do not* be too critical of your old boss. If you do, it will make you sound like a person who blames others and does not accept responsibility. If you were partly at fault, admit it, but quickly take the opportunity to say what you learned from the experience.

Quip

Larger organizations often don't allow employees to give references. If you are worried about a negative reference, this rule may be a great relief to you. Check it out by calling your former employers and finding out their policy.

Sample Answer

"My three former employers will all say I work hard, am very reliable, and am loyal. The reason I left my previous job, however, is the result of what I can only call a personality conflict. While there, I received several promotions, and as my authority increased, there were more conflicts with my boss. Our styles were just not the same. I had no idea the problem was so serious because I was so involved in my work. I have since learned to pay more attention to interpersonal matters. You can call and get a positive reference, but I thought it only fair to tell you. I still respect my ex-boss and am grateful for the experience I gained at that job."

This response could be strengthened by elaborating on the experience gained, particularly any skills learned on the job.

Question #9: "Why Are You Looking for This Sort of Position and Why Here?"

The employer wants to make sure you are not the sort of person who is just looking for any job, anywhere. People who have a good reason to work in a particular job or for a particular organization are seen as more committed and more invested.

In responding to this question, mention your motivations for selecting this career, the special skills you have that the position requires, and any special training or credentials you have which relate to the position. If you have reasons for selecting this organization specifically, be prepared to explain them. Use the research techniques from Step 3 to become as informed as possible.

Sample Answer

An experienced manager could use this type of response, which also uses the Prove-It Technique nicely:

> "I've spent a lot of time considering various careers, and I think that this is the best area for me. This career requires many of my strongest skills, such as my ability to analyze and solve problems. For example, in a previous job, I created a plan that resulted in reducing customer returns of leased equipment by 15 percent. The result was an increase in retained leases of more than $250,000 a year for a plan that cost about $100 to implement. This particular organization seems to be the type that would let me use similar problem-solving skills. It is well-run, growing rapidly, and open to new ideas. Your sales went up 30 percent last year, and you are getting ready to introduce several major new products. If I work hard, I feel I would have the opportunity to stay with the business as it grows and grow with it."

Question #10: "Why Don't You Tell Me About Your Personal Situation?"

A good interviewer will rarely ask this question so directly. More often, interviewers use casual and friendly conversation to get the information they want. In most cases, the interviewer is digging for anything that would indicate you are unstable or undependable.

Other issues may be of concern to an employer as well, often based on assumptions the interviewer has about people with certain characteristics. These beliefs are often irrelevant, and some may seem to be in bad taste or even illegal (see Step 5 for more on this issue). But if the employer wonders whether you can be depended upon, dealing with these doubts is in your own best interest. In responding to a question about your personal situation, always be friendly and positive.

Examples of Appropriate Answers

The following responses address the personal issues that employers are most concerned about.

Young children at home:

> "I have two children, both in school. Child care is no problem because they stay with a good friend."

Single head of household:

> "I'm not married and have two children at home. It is very important to me to have a steady income, so child care is no problem."

Young and single:

> "I'm not married, and if I should marry, that would not change my plans for a full-time career. For now, I can devote my full attention to my career."

Just moved here:

> "I've decided to settle here permanently. I've rented an apartment, and I am looking into buying a house."

Relatives, upbringing:

> "I am one of three children. Both of my parents still live within an hour's flight from here, and I see them several times a year."

Leisure time:

> "My time is family-centered when I'm not working. I'm also active in several community organizations."

All of these responses could be expanded on, but they should give you an idea of the types of approaches you can take with your own answers. The message you want to give is that your personal situation will not hurt your ability to work and could even help it.

Other Frequently Asked Interview Questions

The following list presents some of the questions most often asked by recruiters who interview new graduates at college campuses. Although some of the questions may not apply to your situation, they give you a good idea of the types of questions a trained interviewer might ask you.

1. What are your future vocational plans?
2. In what school activities have you participated? Why? Which did you enjoy the most?
3. How do you spend your free time? What are your hobbies?
4. What type of position most interests you?
5. Why do you think you might like to work for our company?
6. What jobs have you held? How did you get them?
7. What courses did you like best? Least? Why?
8. Why did you choose your particular field of work?
9. How did you spend your vacations while in school?
10. What do you know about our company?
11. What qualifications do you have that make you feel that you will be successful in your field?
12. What extracurricular offices have you held?
13. How do you feel about your family?
14. If you were starting school all over again, what would you do differently?
15. Can you forget your education and start from scratch?
16. How much money do you hope to earn at age ____?
17. Why did you decide to go to the school you attended?
18. What do you think determines a person's progress in a good company?
19. What personal characteristics are necessary for success in your chosen field?
20. Why do you think you would like this particular type of job?
21. Tell me about your home life during the time you were growing up.
22. Do you prefer working with others or by yourself?

23. What kind of boss do you prefer?
24. Can you take instructions without feeling upset?
25. How did previous employers treat you?
26. What have you learned from some of the jobs you have held?
27. What interests you about our product or service?
28. What was your record in military service?
29. Did you ever change your major field of interest? Why?
30. Give me an example of when you did the best work you were capable of.
31. What do you know about opportunities in the field in which you are trained?
32. How long do you expect to work?
33. Have you ever had any difficulty getting along with fellow students and faculty? Fellow workers?
34. What was most difficult about school or your last job?
35. What size city do you prefer?
36. How do you usually spend your weekends?
37. Have you had any serious illness or injury?
38. Are you willing to go where the company sends you?
39. What job in our company would you choose if you were entirely free to do so?
40. Is it an effort for you to be tolerant of persons with a background and interests different from yours?
41. What types of books do you read?
42. Do you have plans for further education?
43. What types of people seem to rub you the wrong way?
44. What jobs have you enjoyed the most? The least? Why?
45. What are your own special abilities?
46. Would you prefer a large or a small company? Why?
47. What is your idea of how industry operates today?

48. How do you feel about overtime work?

49. What are the disadvantages of your chosen field?

50. What have you done that shows initiative and willingness to work?

STEP 5: Handle Tough Interview Situations with Confidence

We all have things about ourselves and our past that could pose a problem for some employers. You may have "too much" or "too little" education or training or gaps in your work history. You may be "too old" or "too young" or have other characteristics that concern some employers. Many of these things you can't change, but it is your job to assure employers that they shouldn't be a concern.

The Question of Illegal Questions

Employers can *ask* almost anything they want in an interview. They can ask offensive questions, personal questions, and even just plain dumb questions. They just can't *use* that information to hire one person over another based on certain criteria, such as race, gender, or religion.

As a job seeker, it's important to realize that most questions, even ones that might seem inappropriate, are probably intended to find out whether you will be a good employee. That *is* a legitimate concern for an employer, and you have the responsibility of letting the employer know you will be a good choice.

There are situations, however, where an interviewer's questions *are* offensive. They may be offensive in the way they are asked or because of the type of questions they are. If that is the case, you probably should reconsider wanting to work for such a person. You might even report that employer to the authorities.

Know the Laws That Protect You from Discrimination

Two major laws come into play in cases of hiring discrimination:

- Title VII of the Civil Rights Act makes discrimination on the basis of race, gender, religion, or national origin illegal in hiring discussions.

- The Americans with Disabilities Act, which was put into effect in 1992, requires that an employer provide an equal opportunity for an individual with a disability to participate in the job application process and to be considered for a job.

Keep in mind that specific jobs might require an answer to some questions that might appear to be illegal for other jobs. For example, firefighters need to be in good physical condition because they may be required to climb a ladder carrying 100 or more pounds; therefore strength and health-related questions are acceptable in interviews for firefighters. Bartenders need to be at least 21 years old, so the interviewer can ask about age when interviewing a bartender. In general, however, an employer is not allowed to consider information that is not related to a person's ability to do the job.

Quip

If you think you have been discriminated against in the job hiring process, visit the U.S. Equal Employment Opportunity Commission Web site at www.eeoc.gov. It will give you guidelines for determining whether discrimination has occurred and instructions for filing a complaint.

Specific Problem Interview Situations

This section deals with issues most people experience and that are often (but not always) legitimate issues for an employer to explore. No doubt many, if not most, of us would resent that employers would even consider such things as race, age, religion, national origin, child care, and other personal matters in evaluating people for employment. But some employers do consider these things, despite the fact it is unfair or even illegal to do so. Just remember that most employers simply want to be assured that you will stay on the job for a reasonable length of time and do well.

Gaps in Your Work History

About one out of five people in the workforce experience some unemployment each year, and most bosses have experienced it themselves.

If you have a legitimate reason for major gaps in your work history, such as going to school or having a child, tell the interviewer in a matter-of-fact way; don't apologize or act embarrassed about it. You could, however, add details about a related activity you did during that period that would strengthen your qualifications for the job.

Quip

It may help to refer to dates in years rather than months, for example "from 2003 to 2005" rather than "from November 2003 to June 2005." This is still truthful and avoids showing short gaps in your work history.

Being Fired

Lots of people get fired, often for reasons that don't reflect on their ability to do the job in question. Of course, if you were fired for just cause, you need to learn from the experience and change your behavior or consider another career. However, there are ways to address this in an interview.

> **Quip**
>
> If you have been fired, it is also important to negotiate with your previous employer about what he or she will say when giving you a reference. These negotiations can help offset a negative past employer who may simply have had a personality conflict with you.

Many employers tell me they will not hire someone unless they know why the person left his or her last job. The good news here is that many employers have been fired themselves and are sympathetic. If you have a reasonable explanation, many interviewers will understand. The best policy is usually to tell the truth of what happened in your past job in an objective way, and then quickly turn to presenting the skills you have to do the job under discussion.

Job History Unrelated to Your Current Job Objective

Don't worry, if your past experience was a real barrier, you wouldn't have been invited for an interview in the first place. Just emphasize your adaptive and transferable skills and how they relate to the job you are discussing. For instance, a teacher who wants to become a real estate agent could cite superior communication skills and an ability to motivate students in the classroom (convincing an eight-year-old to do math homework may be even harder than persuading an adult to buy a house). Look up the job descriptions of your old jobs and the one you want now, and find skills they have in common.

Recently Moved

Employers may be concerned that someone who has recently moved to an area does not have roots there and may soon leave. If you are new to the area, make sure the employer knows you are there to stay. Provide a simple statement that presents you as a stable member of the community. It may be helpful to mention any family or friends who live nearby.

Military Experience

Employers who have not had military experience themselves often have misconceptions about those who have. Some of the stereotypes of military people can work in your favor, however. Here are some suggestions for making the most of your military experience:

- Employers want people who can get along with others. Some people assume military personnel are overly aggressive. You can easily handle this stereotype by being friendly or emphasizing community service.
- Employers need people who work well in teams and solve problems. The truth is that the military has been training with team cooperation and creative problem solving for years. Try to offer a few examples of your teamwork and problem-solving skills in action.
- Employers may wonder why you left or assume that you don't have "civilian" skills. Each year more than 300,000 people leave the military. In most cases, ex-military people have benefited from excellent and expensive training, are more educated than the average person their age, and have had far more management experience than the average job seeker. These are good points to emphasize.

To reinforce your abilities as a civilian worker, avoid wearing military dress and accessories and using any military jargon. Be sure to emphasize those qualities that are important to all employers, such as discipline, responsibility, and dependability.

The Turtling Technique

Like a turtle on its back, a problem is a problem only if you leave it that way. By turning it over ("turtling" it), you can turn a perceived disadvantage into an advantage. Take a look at these examples:

- Too old: "I am a very stable worker requiring very little training. I have been dependable all my life, and I am at a point in my career where I don't plan on changing jobs. I still have 10 years of working until I plan on retiring. How long has the average young person stayed here?"
- Too young: "I don't have any bad work habits to break, so I can be quickly trained to do things the way you want. I plan on working hard to get established. I'll also work for less money than a more experienced worker."

Negative References

Most employers do not contact your previous employers unless you are being seriously considered for the job. If you fear that one of your previous employers may not give you a positive reference, here are some things you can do:

- List someone other than your former supervisor as a reference. Find someone who knows your work and who will put in a good word for you.
- Discuss the issue in advance with your previous employer and negotiate what he or she will say. Even if it's not good, at least you know what they are likely to say and can prepare potential employers in advance.
- Get a written letter of reference. Presenting a letter of reference ensures that you know what is said about you.

Criminal Record

In the United States most employers are not allowed to consider an arrest record in a hiring decision. Being *arrested* and being *convicted* of a crime are two different things, however. Current employment laws *do* allow an employer to ask for and get information about felony convictions and to use it in making certain hiring decisions. After all, few employers would hire an accountant who had been convicted of stealing money.

> **Quip**
>
> Certain employers can consider certain types of arrest records in making hiring decisions as well. For example, few daycare centers would hire a person who has been arrested for child abuse whether that person had been convicted or not.

If you have an arrest or conviction record that an employer has a legal right to inquire about, you should avoid jobs where your record would be a negative. As always, your interview should emphasize what you *can* do rather than what you can't. If you choose your career direction wisely and present a convincing argument that you can do the job well, many employers will ultimately overlook previous mistakes. As you prove yourself and gain good work experience, your distant past becomes less and less important.

Background Checks

Many employers screen applicants before hiring. Screening is more common for jobs where theft can be a problem, for jobs that involve work with children, and for positions that require driving. Background checks may include drug screening, credit history, criminal history, verification of education and training, and checks with past employers. In some cases an employer will not consider hiring anyone who does not agree to these background checks.

If you have a serious problem in your background, avoid careers and jobs where your past would be an issue or use job search methods that are less likely to require this information as part of the screening process.

Sensitive Questions About Your Personal Situation

Because many people consider the issues in this section—such as age, race, and gender—inappropriate for an employer to consider when making a decision to hire, employers are much more likely to use indirect questions regarding these concerns.

Most employers will hire someone who convinces them that he or she can do the job well. Your handling of the interview can assure the interviewer that you do not fit a stereotype. But in order to prevent misconceptions, it's helpful to know what these stereotypes might be and address them.

"Too Old"

Older workers—particularly those over 50—have a harder time finding new jobs in the labor market, despite their often high qualifications. This group includes a lot of workers who have lost jobs due to layoffs, downsizing, and other reasons not related to performance.

Employers may be concerned that older workers haven't kept up with their skills or with the latest technology, or that older workers will expect better pay and are more likely to leave the job for a better offer.

The key to confronting these concerns is to present your wealth of experience and maturity as an advantage rather than a disadvantage. Emphasize your loyalty to previous employers, and highlight accomplishments that occurred over a period of time. Confront the issue of compensation by convincing employers how you will increase profits or save the company money in the long run.

If you have more than 15 years of work experience, emphasize your more recent work activities that best support your ability to do the job. You don't have to provide many details on your earlier work history unless doing so is clearly to your advantage.

Quip

Competition for high-paying jobs is intense. Unemployment statistics indicate that the more you make, the longer your job search is likely to be. A rule of thumb is that it takes one month per $10,000 in annual pay to find a new job. If you make $50,000 a year, plan on it taking five months to find a replacement job at that level of income.

Overqualified/Too Much Experience

It doesn't make sense that you could have too much experience, but some employers may think so. They fear you will not be satisfied with the job that is available and will soon leave for a better one.

Go out of your way to assure the interviewer that you aren't a job hopper. Maintain high enthusiasm for the organization's future, and present ways you could grow in this position. Suggest how you could solve long-term problems, build profit, and use your experience to help out in other ways.

"Too Young"

Younger people need to present their youth as an asset rather than a liability. Often young people are willing to work for less money, accept less desirable tasks, work longer or less convenient hours, or do other things that a more experienced worker might not want to do. If this is true, you should say so in the interview. Emphasize the time and dedication you put into school projects. Above all, conduct yourself with maturity and show some enthusiasm and energy.

Another advantage that many younger people have is being more comfortable with newer technology than their elders. This important advantage helps many younger workers gain an edge over their older, but less tech-savvy competitors.

New Graduate/Not Enough Experience

If this is your first real job, be sure to stress any technical expertise you've acquired in school and emphasize the adaptive skills you identified in Step 2 that would help you overcome a lack of experience. Also remember to treat any coursework directly related to the job your interviewing for as "work experience," especially if it involved hands-on training or internships.

> **Quip**
>
> New graduates should note that small employers are where the action is. The Endicott Report from Northwestern University found that small- to mid-sized companies tend to be the most active recruiters. Smaller organizations are often more open to letting you take on new projects and directions, which can lead to more rapid advancement as well.

Issues Related to Women

Despite the great progress women have made in most career fields, some employers and some career areas still present barriers to them. According to a survey conducted by the Society of Human Resource Management, some employers still have concerns about working mothers, the acceptance of women in nontraditional roles, and the "glass ceiling" that seems to prevent women from achieving the highest levels of management.

For Carol Price, an educator and lecturer with Career Track, much of this gender bias can be dealt with by establishing your equal status the second you walk in the room. "Once you do that, I really believe gender issues go away," she says. How do you establish equal status? Simply look like you belong at the interview. "That means my head is held up, my shoulders are back, I walk in without hesitation, and I put my hand out," says Price. "A handshake was originally devised to prove we were weaponless. In a job interview, that translates to 'you and I are equal in value'."

Child Care

A *Harvard Business Review* study documented that "on average, working mothers put in an 84-hour work week between their homes and their jobs." In other words, a working mother essentially holds down two full-time jobs. For women with or likely to have children, the number one task is to assure the interviewer that they don't intend to abandon their families but do intend to devote the necessary time to the job.

> **Quip**
>
> Interestingly enough, women employers are just as concerned as male employers are about a woman's family status. Employers of both genders assume that a woman is more likely to have child-related problems and want to be certain that these will not become a work-related problem.

Handling questions about child care is simply a matter of turning the situation into a positive. For example, illustrate your management skills by describing how you handled work responsibilities when your child was ill and you needed to be at home. But still be prepared to back up your loyalty claims with actual numbers of days missed from previous jobs.

Issues Related to Men

Just as with women (but in different ways), men are expected to behave in certain ways and quietly accept the limitations imposed on them. For example, men are often expected to have steady employment and not take time off for raising a family or caring for elderly parents.

Even so, there are few situations where being a man will work against you, particularly if you have a good work history. Though issues like the possibility of becoming a stay-at-home dad certainly exist, they seldom come up in interviews because the stereotype works the other way.

Sexual Preference

The Society for Human Resource Management survey reveals that "In our traditional, conservative culture, managers have deeply ingrained biases and fears of gay and lesbian employees."

Although I would advocate directly attacking stereotypes in other categories, I recommend the military's "don't ask, don't tell" policy in the case of sexuality. The risks of divulging such personal information are too great to bring up in an interview, and your sexuality is not something you should have to discuss in a job interview anyway. As with all stereotypes, an employer who wouldn't hire you on such grounds is not one you are likely to want to work for.

Racial or Ethnic Minorities

The good news is that most employers fairly consider hiring a person based on his or her qualifications. In fact, many employers go out of their way to give minorities fair consideration through active recruiting.

The bad news is that some employers are still less likely to hire a qualified minority because of negative stereotypes. Unfortunately, you are not likely to know which employers are being fair and which are not. Your best bet is to assume that the interviewer is being fair and will consider hiring you based on your skills and abilities, and then focus on those skills in the interview.

> **Quip**
>
> Limited English proficiency is another problem for many employers, and you will need to address this issue if it applies to you. Suggest that you are a good worker and are learning English rapidly, and consider how you can help the employer provide better service to those who speak your native language.

Disability-Related Issues

Biases against people with disabilities continue to influence hiring decisions, despite the Americans with Disabilities Act. According to the Society for Human Resource Management survey, many respondents indicated that accommodating employees with disabilities presents difficulties for their organizations. They say that organizations worry about time off for illnesses and medical treatments and the cost of making special accommodations.

Assuming you would not seek a job that you could not or should not do, then you don't actually have a disability related to doing a particular job at all. Your goal is to convince employers of that fact by highlighting your skills and providing proof of your successes.

Some Other Tricky Questions

The questions that follow are all legal, and they give you the opportunity to let an employer know that your situation will not be a problem. Your good answer to one of these questions lets you put an employer's concerns to rest.

- **How long have you been looking for another job?** Never give an actual timeframe. Casually reply, "Time isn't a factor because I'm searching for the position that best matches my skills and goals."
- **What type of person would *you* hire for this position?** There really is only one answer to this question: "I'd hire someone who has the skills and experience to handle the job. In other words, someone like me."
- **Why do you want to leave your present job (or why did you leave past jobs)?** Do not complain about your past jobs or employers. Doing so will make you seem negative. More appropriate answers include this being a step in your career plans or wanting a better job location.

Quip

Most of us are not comfortable with silence, so when the interviewer says nothing but maintains eye contact, most job seekers feel pressured into either giving more details or starting another topic altogether. Yet the best way to handle silence is by remaining quiet and appearing pleasant. In the interest of time, the interviewer eventually asks the next question.

- **How do you normally handle criticism?** Suggest that you are eager to correct any mistakes or misunderstandings the minute they arise and that you see criticism as an opportunity to learn and grow (or a welcome challenge to do better next time).
- **What do you do for fun in your spare time?** This question not only confirms how much time (or overtime) you are willing to devote to your work, but it also confirms those things the employer can't legally ask, such as whether you have a family, whether you attend church, and so on. Try to emphasize activities that complement your desirable personality traits or skills.
- **Describe your typical day.** Naturally, leave out the fact that you aren't a morning person. Instead use this opportunity to advertise how well you organize yourself and conceptualize long-term projects. Also discuss how good it makes you feel to get a lot done during the day and know you've done a good job.

Above all, remember to be confident. Even if an employer shows some initial concern, your confidence can convince them otherwise.

STEP 6: Follow Up

Following up on an interview can mean the difference between being unemployed or underemployed and getting the job you want fast. When you get home from the interview, do the following:

- **Make notes on the interview.** While it is fresh in your mind, jot down key points you'd like to remember.
- **Schedule your follow-up.** If you agreed to call back at a specific date and time, be sure to mark it on your calendar.
- **Send your thank-you note.** Send an e-mail thank-you that very same day, and follow this with a thank-you note through regular mail.
- **Call when you said you would.** If a job opening exists and you want it, say so and explain why. If no job opening exists, say you enjoyed the visit and would like to stay in touch during your job search. This is also a good time to ask for the names of anyone else with whom you might speak about a position for a person with your skills and experience.

The Importance of Thank-You Notes

When used properly, thank-you notes can help you create a positive impression with employers that more formal correspondence often can't.

When to Send Thank-You Notes—and Why

1. **Before an interview:** You can send a less formal note before an interview, usually by e-mail, simply thanking someone for being willing to see you. This note also serves as a way to confirm the date and time of the scheduled interview.
2. **After an interview:** The best time to send a thank-you note is right after an interview, or at least within 24 hours. Doing so creates a positive impression and keeps you at the forefront of the employer's mind (hopefully ahead of the other candidates). It also gives you a chance to get in the last word—to include a subtle reminder of why you're the best candidate for the job. The following is an example of such a note.

August 11, 20XX

Dear Mr. O'Beel,

Thank you for the opportunity to interview for the position available in your production department. I want you to know that this is the sort of job I have been looking for, and I am enthusiastic about the possibility of working for you.

Now that we have spoken, I know that I have both the experience and skills to fit nicely into your organization and to be productive quickly. The process improvements I implemented at Logistics, Inc., increased their productivity 34%, and I'm confident that I could do the same for you.

Thanks again for the interview; I enjoyed the visit.

Sara Smith

(505) 665-0090

3. **Whenever anyone helps you in your job search:** Send a thank-you e-mail or note to anyone who helps you during your job search. This group of people includes those who give you referrals, people who provide advice, or those who are supportive during your search. You never know when you will need their help again in the future. The following shows an example of this type of note.

October 31, 20XX
2234 Riverbed Ave.
Philadelphia, PA 17963

Ms. Helen A. Colcord
Henderson and Associates, Inc.
1801 Washington Blvd., Suite 1201
Philadelphia, PA 17963

Dear Ms. Colcord,

Thank you for sharing your time with me so generously yesterday. I really appreciated talking to you about your career field.

The information you shared with me increased my desire to work in such an area. Your advice has already proven helpful—I have an appointment to meet with Robert Hopper on Friday.

In case you think of someone else who might need a person like me, I'm enclosing another resume and JIST Card.

Sincerely,

Debbie Childs

Seven Quick Tips for Writing Thank-You Notes

Use these tips to help you write your thank-you notes:

1. **Decide whether to use e-mail or regular mail.** Use e-mail to get a letter out quickly. Use regular mail if there's no rush and if you sense that the other person would appreciate the formality of a nice business letter. Of course, it probably won't hurt to do both.
2. **Use quality paper and envelopes.** Most stationery stores have thank-you note cards and envelopes in a variety of styles. A blank card or simple "Thank You" on the front will do.
3. **Handwritten or computer-printed is acceptable.** If your handwriting is good, writing them is perfectly acceptable and can be a nice touch. If not, they can be word-processed.
4. **Use a formal salutation.** Unless you've already met the person you're writing to and are on a first name basis, use "Dear Ms. Smith" or "Ms. Smith," rather than the less formal "Dear Pam."

Quip

If you send a formal letter or thank-you note as an e-mail attachment, make sure it is in a universal format such as Microsoft Word, WordPerfect, Rich Text, Adobe PDF, or HTML. Always mention the format in your e-mail message as well.

5. **Keep the note short and friendly.** Remember, the note is a thank-you for what someone else did, not a hard-sell pitch for what you want. Make sure, though, to give a subtle, gentle reminder of your skills or other qualifications that are relevant to the job. As appropriate, be specific about when you will next contact the person.
6. **Sign it.** Avoid initials and make your signature legible (unless you're being hired for your creative talents, in which case a wacky-looking, illegible signature could be a plus!).
7. **Send it right away.** Write and send your note no later than 24 hours after you make your contact while the details are fresh in your mind.

Quip

Always send a note or e-mail after an interview, even if it didn't go well. It can't hurt (unless, of course, it's full of typos... or calls the interviewer names).

More Sample Thank-You Notes

Following are two more samples of thank-you notes to help you structure your own. Notice that they are short and friendly and typically mention that the writer will follow up in the future—a key element of a successful job search campaign.

April 22, 20XX

Dear Mr. Nelson,

Thank you so much for seeing me while I was in town last week. I am grateful for your kindness, the interview, and all the information you gave me.

I will call you once again in a few weeks to see if any openings have developed in your marketing research department's planned expansion.

Appreciatively,

Phil Simons

Voice mail: (633) 299-3034

E-mail: psimons@email.com

July 26, 20XX

Dear Ms. Bailey,

Thank you for the interview for the auditor's job last week.

I appreciate the information you gave me and the opportunity to interview with John Petero. He asked me for a transcript, which I am forwarding today.

Working in my field of finance in a respected firm such as Barry Productions appeals to me greatly. I appreciate your consideration and look forward to hearing from you.

Sincerely,

Dan Rehling
Cell phone: 404-991-3443

Follow-Up Letters

In a few cases, a longer or more detailed letter is better to provide additional information or to present a proposal. If no job was available, you could submit a proposal that would *create* a job and state what you would do to make hiring you pay off. Tell employers what you could accomplish and they may just make a new position for you.

You can also use a post-interview letter to address any concerns the employer may have had during the interview. Once you have put the employer's concerns to rest, reinforce your interest in the job, reiterate that you would be a good match, and suggest a good date for following up with a phone call or second interview.

Follow-Up Phone Calls and E-mail

Most employers are impressed with a job seeker who follows up by phone or e-mail, because most job seekers are not that assertive and enthusiastic. A phone call is more personal and effective but can be supported by e-mail as appropriate. Use these tips to improve your results when following up:

- **Get a time.** Before you leave the interview, ask when would be a good time to contact the interviewer again and note that time on your schedule.
- **Don't forget.** Call or e-mail back on the day and at the time the interviewer suggested. By then, he or she will have received your thank-you note.
- **If you want the job, say so.** Tell the interviewer why you want it and why you think it is a good fit for you and for the organization.
- **Be brave; stay in contact on a regular basis.** If the employer doesn't have an opening now, ask to stay in touch. Make it clear that you are interested in working for them and would like to call or e-mail them back on a regular basis to see if any positions become available.
- **Ask for referrals.** Each time you contact employers, ask whether they know of anyone else who might have a job opening for someone with your skills.

And remember that even if you don't get the job offer, your enthusiasm and attention to detail could make you a prime candidate for future positions in the organization.

STEP 7: Negotiate Your Way to a Fair Salary

Congratulations, they want to hire you. Most job seekers accept the first offer thrown their way because they're afraid they will kill their chance at the job if they try to negotiate. But while nodding politely and saying "That's fine" is the path of least resistance, it's often the path to the least income as well.

Four Negotiation Mistakes to Avoid

Experts cite these strategic mistakes that novice negotiators make:

1. **Lack of persistence:** Just because the employer doesn't accept your counter offer immediately doesn't mean they won't eventually. Hang in there.

2. **Impatience:** The process can take a while. Take some time to think and let the employer mull over your numbers.
3. **Going in too low:** Setting the bar low usually means the other side won't go much higher.
4. **Lack of research:** Get the facts that back up the numbers, and know what you are worth.

Farr's Four Rules of Salary Negotiation

Here are four basic rules of salary negotiation that you should keep in mind.

Rule #1: Never talk money until after an employer decides he or she wants you.

Early in the hiring process, many employers want to know how much you expect to be paid so they can screen out those applicants whose salary expectations are too high. So always defer the question until it's part of an offer.

If the topic of salary comes up before a job offer is made, avoid discussing any specific dollar amounts. Instead try one of the following tactics:

- "I'm very interested in the position, and my salary would be negotiable."
- "Tell me what you have in mind for the salary range."
- "I am interested in the job and would consider any reasonable offer you might make."

With a bit of luck, stall tactics such as these will get the employer to tell *you* the salary range without you having to commit to anything.

Rule #2: Know in advance the probable salary range.

Approaching an interview without being prepared for discussions of pay is not wise. Although you will have to do a bit of research, knowing what an employer is likely to pay is essential in salary negotiations.

The trick is to think in terms of a wide *range* in salary, rather than a particular number. Find out the general range that jobs of this sort are likely to pay in your area by asking those who work in similar jobs, finding the information online, or visiting the library.

Salary Information Resources

In order to determine the salary you are willing to accept, investigate the salary range someone with your skills and experience can expect to receive. The following Web sites can help you, as can your personal network, local librarian, and local job search centers.

- **Abbott, Langer & Associates (www.abbott-langer.com):** This site contains current statistics for more than 450 benchmark jobs and from more than 8,000 participating organizations.
- **JobStar Salary Information (jobstar.org/tools/salary/):** Provides 300 links to general and profession-specific salary surveys. Take some time to explore salary negotiation strategies and test your own salary IQ.
- **Salary Expert (www.salaryexpert.com):** Find free regional salary reports by selecting your job title and then your ZIP code or city.

Rule #3: Always bracket your stated salary range to begin within the employer's probable salary range and end a bit above what you expect to settle for.

Suppose that the employer is expecting to pay someone about $25,000 a year. Your research indicates that most jobs of this type pay between $22,000 and $29,000 a year. You could say you were hoping for $30,000, but in many cases, this will probably eliminate you from consideration. Alternatively you could say you would take $22,000, at which point you could get hired at $22,000 a year (making that response the most expensive two seconds in your entire life), or the employer could go looking for someone who feels they are worth more than that.

Instead, you want to bracket the range, staying a little bit on the high side. In the above example, you figured that the probable range for the salary would be from $22,000 to $29,000. You could cover this range by saying, "I was looking for a salary in the mid- to upper twenties." You can use the same strategy for any salary bracket you may be considering. For example, if you want $28,000 a year and their range is $25,000 to $33,000, you could say "A salary in the high twenties to mid-thirties."

Talking in terms of a salary range that extends a bit above what the employer was likely to consider not only gives you the option of negotiating your salary when it really matters, but if you *are* offered the job, you are likely to be offered a little more than what the employer originally intended.

Rule #4: Never say no to a job offer either before it is made or within 24 hours afterward.

Many job seekers don't realize that their response to salary can eliminate them from further consideration. Showing disappointment at an interviewer's initial salary proposal could cause that person to keep looking for someone who would be delighted with the pay.

Quip

Web and newspaper ads are notorious for demanding that respondents list their salary requirements. If you feel that a particular job is a good bet, indicate that your "salary requirements are open to negotiation."

To avoid losing the job before the interview is over, you might consider countering a lower-than-hoped-for offer by saying something like, "That is somewhat lower than I had hoped, but this position does sound very interesting. If I were to consider this offer, what sorts of things could I do to quickly become more valuable to this organization?"

Remember that a discussion of salary is not necessarily a job offer. More often, it is an attempt to screen you out of consideration. The key is to continue to delay discussion of pay until it really matters.

What to Say When It Really Matters

If the employer has offered you the job and is ready to discuss pay, remember the most important rule of salary negotiation: *The one who speaks first loses.* In other words, let them open up the bidding. The employer is likely to make a reasonable first offer, but may offer more if pressed.

If the Offer Is Not What You Want

Thank them for the offer and politely ask for two days to think about it. Leave and see if you change your mind. If not, call back and say, in effect:

> "I've given your offer considerable thought and feel that I just can't take it at the salary you've offered. Is there any way that I could be paid more, in the range of ___________________?"

This is not a time to play games, so don't reject the offer unless you really are willing to keep looking. If the employer really wants you, however, he or she may be willing to meet your terms. If the employer cannot meet your salary needs, say thank you again, and let him or her know you are interested in future openings within your salary range.

Quip

No matter what you do, never turn down a job offer until you have given yourself a day to think it over.

The Offer Is Reasonable

Accepting a reasonable offer right away can be a mistake. Remember first that money isn't everything. Be sure you are happy with the job description, the work environment, the possibilities for advancement, and all other aspects of the job. Also, discussing the offer with others (especially family) before saying yes is wise. Most employers expect applicants to take some time to consider offers and may be a little surprised if you don't.

You Want the Job—Time to Negotiate

If you do want the job and the offer is acceptable or close, it is okay to discuss this with the employer face-to-face. Here are some tips for handling this delicate situation.

Know Your Acceptable Range in Advance

You've let the employer suggest a figure, but before you make a counteroffer there's something you need to know: How much cash and fringe benefits will it take to make you accept the position?

Michael Schatzki, owner of the New Jersey–based Negotiation Dynamics, recommends that you know the very least you would be willing to accept and the most you could reasonably hope for. You can negotiate a higher rate, but if the offer falls below your minimum, continue job hunting.

Play the Negotiation Game

The first number the interviewer mentions is rarely the highest possible salary offer. But laughing and saying, "You and I both know you can do better," is not good negotiating etiquette. So when the initial figure is mentioned, your first reaction should be silence. This lets the interviewer know that you are considering the offer and are not entirely satisfied with it. In fact, a study by Haldane Associates (an executive search firm) has discovered that in more than 50 percent of all situations where silence is used, the interviewers cough up a higher figure without further discussion.

Quip

Get inside information on salary negotiation at Quintessential Careers' Salary Negotiation Tutorial (www.quintcareers.com/salary_negotiation.html). You'll find tips on getting the best possible salary, turning unacceptable offers into acceptable ones, handling salary discussions during an interview, and more.

Recognize the Final Offer…Then Make the Most of It

Again, you don't want to lose an acceptable job offer by demanding more. Some employers will see your resistance to accepting their offer as a sign of not being happy with it. So let them know that you *do* want the job, if that is the case. Do not delay your decision to accept: Say yes once the offer is acceptable to you.

If the salary is lower than you would accept, there are other things you might negotiate with an employer. For example:

- Stock options
- Vacation time
- Performance bonuses
- Flex time (work four 10-hour days and take Fridays off, work 10 a.m. to 6:00 p.m. to avoid rush hours, job-share, or telecommute)
- Company car
- Geographic location, if there is more than one office

Before you shake hands to seal the deal, feel free to ask for 24 hours to think it over. Don't worry, such careful thought and responsible consideration will earn the respect of a potential employer.

In Closing

Sixty minutes. That's usually all the time you have to convince an employer to hire you. The good news is that an hour is all the time your competition has as well. The difference is that you've read this book (or skipped ahead to the last page), which means you should be better prepared than most other applicants. Still, just in case you *did* skip ahead, I'll close this book with a few final tips:

- **Know yourself.** Know what your skills are and be prepared to give examples to back them up. Quantify your achievements whenever possible, and don't be afraid to say you're the best candidate for the job (and why).
- **Know the employer.** Do your research. Understand the industry and the direction the organization is headed. Be prepared to discuss salary ranges as well.

- **Turn negatives into positives.** Interviewers are looking for potential problems. Your job is to assure them that your issues won't become their issues.
- **Don't forget to follow up.** Those thank-you cards and phone calls can make a big difference.
- **Remember, no matter what questions interviewers ask, the underlying question is always, "Why should I hire you?"** Be prepared to give them lots of good reasons.

I wish you the best of luck.

Appendix

How to Get More Interviews

Although this book's focus is on improving your interviewing skills, you won't be able to put those skills to work unless you get the interviews to begin with. This appendix describes a few of the job search methods that can help you land interviews before anyone else ever knows there's an opening.

You can be considered for a job opening long before it is advertised. In fact, most jobs are never advertised because someone like you gets there before the job needs to be. Employers prefer to hire people they already know or who are referred to them by someone they know. Many are willing to talk to you even before they have a job opening if you approach them in the right way. The result: Half of all jobs are filled before a formal job opening would even be announced.

> **Quip**
>
> The most important job search rule of all: Don't wait until the job is open before asking for an interview!

The Two Best Ways to Find Jobs and Get Interviews

The best time to search for a job is before anyone else knows about it. For this reason, these jobs are sometimes referred to as the hidden job market or the networked job market. The key to finding jobs in this market is to meet people who can hire you before a job is even available.

Job Search Method #1: Develop a Network of Contacts

Studies find that 60 percent of all people located their jobs through a lead provided by a friend, relative, or acquaintance. The people you know are your number one source of job leads. The key is to develop and expand your list of contacts, a process otherwise known as networking. Here's how it works:

1. **Make lists of people you know.** Make a thorough list of anyone you are friendly with and another separate list of all your relatives. Next, think of other groups of people that you have something in common with, such as former co-workers or classmates, former employers, neighbors, and other groups. By the time you are done, you will probably have a list of hundreds of people who will help you if you ask them.

2. **Contact each person in your list in a systematic way.** Obviously, some people will be more helpful than others, but any one of them might help you find a job lead. Be sure to keep track of who you contacted and to send thank-you notes to the people who help.

3. **Present yourself well.** Begin with your friends and relatives. Call and tell them you are looking for a job and need their help. Be as clear as possible about the type of employment you want and the skills and qualifications you have.

> **Quip**
>
> Job seekers get more interviews by using the phone than by any other method. For example, you can use the phone to call people you already know to get referrals, follow up by calling leads you got, stay in touch with prospective employers, and make cold calls to ask for interviews.

4. **Ask your contacts for leads.** It is possible that your contacts will know of a job opening that interests you. If so, get the details and get right on it! More likely, however, they will not, so you should ask them if they can put you in touch with someone who does.

5. **Contact these referrals and ask them the same questions.** From each person you contact, try to get names of two other people you might contact. Doing this consistently can extend your network by hundreds of people. Eventually, one of them will hire you or refer you to someone who will!

The JIST Card®—A Quick Ticket to Job Leads

Look at the sample cards that follow—they are JIST Cards, and they get results. Computer printed or even neatly written on a 3-by-5–inch card, JIST Cards act as a kind of mini resume. About 80 percent of employers say they would be willing to interview the person behind the JIST Card, even if they did not have a job opening available.

> Sandy Nolan
>
> Position: General Office/Clerical
>
> Message: (512) 232-9213
>
> More than two years of work experience plus one year of training in office practices. Type 55 wpm, trained in word processing, post general ledger, have good interpersonal skills, and get along with most people. Can meet deadlines and handle pressure well.
>
> Willing to work any hours.
>
> Organized, honest, reliable, and hardworking.

Juanita Rodriguez

Message: (639) 361-1754
Email: jrodriguez@email.com

Position: Warehouse Management

Six years of experience plus two years of formal business course work. Have supervised a staff as large as 16 people and warehousing operations covering over two acres and valued at more than $14,000,000. Automated inventory operations resulting in a 30% increase in turnover and estimated annual savings of more than $250,000. Working knowledge of accounting, computer systems, time and motion studies, and advanced inventory management systems.

Will work any hours.

Responsible, hardworking, and can solve problems.

You can easily create JIST Cards on a computer and print them on card stock you can buy at any office supply store. Or have a few hundred printed cheaply by a local quick print shop. Your can write your own JIST card in 8 easy steps:

1. **Type your name at the top of the card.** You can center it and use bold text to make it stand out, as you would on a resume.
2. **Give two ways for the employer to contact you.** Space down a few lines and left-align this information. Generally, all you will need to include is your daytime phone number or cell phone number and your e-mail address.
3. **Give a broad job objective.** Space down another line or two and left-align this information. A broad objective will allow you to be considered for many jobs.
4. **List your years of experience.** Space down again and add one sentence that summarizes how long you have been working in this field.
5. **Detail your education and training.** In the same paragraph, add a sentence that tells what degrees, certifications, diplomas, and other relevant training you have.
6. **Showcase your job-related skills.** Still in the same paragraph, add up to four sentences that tell what you can do and how well you can do it. Be sure to include accomplishments and numbers to support them. (See Step 2 for help identifying these skills.)

7. **State your availability and preferred working arrangements.** If applicable, space down and add a sentence that states any special availability you might have, such as "interested in part-time work," or "available with two weeks' notice."

8. **End with your key adaptive skills.** Space down a few more lines and add one last sentence that tells what personality traits you have that make you a good employee.

Quip

Most jobs are with small employers. In fact, organizations with fewer than 250 employees employ about 72 percent of all U.S. workers and are the source for 75 percent of the new jobs created each year.

Attach a JIST Card to your resume. Give them to friends, relatives, and other contacts and ask them to pass the cards along to others who might know of an opening. Enclose them in thank-you notes after interviews. Leave them with employers as a business card. However you get them in circulation, you may be surprised at how well they work.

Job Search Method #2: Contact Employers Directly

It takes more courage, but making direct contact with an employer can not only expand your network, but it can lead directly to interviews as well. You can use the *Yellow Pages* to find potential employers. Use the index to find organizations that you think could use your skills and start calling.

Using the Telephone to Get Interviews

Once you get used to it, making direct contacts by phone is easy and effective. Most employers don't mind talking to a person they might be interested in hiring. Because most phone calls take only a minute or two, you can easily make personal contact with more than 20 employers in one morning.

The primary goal of a phone contact is to get an interview. To increase your chances, you need to practice asking for one and have a phone script prepared in advance. Don't be afraid of rejection, and do be prepared to ask for an interview three times. Employers often assume that such a determined person will show the same persistence on the job.

Quip

Instead of calling, you could try just walking into a business or organization that interests you and asking to speak to the person in charge. Just remember to ask for an interview even if there are no current openings.

Call each organization and ask to speak to the person who is most likely to hire or supervise you—typically the manager of the business or a department head—*not* the personnel or human resources manager. The following sample telephone script can give you ideas about what to say:

> "Hello. My name is Pam Nykanen. I am interested in a position in hotel management. I have four years of experience in sales, catering, and accounting with a 300-room hotel. I also have an associate degree in hotel management, plus one year of experience with the Brady Culinary Institute. During my employment, I helped double revenues from meetings and conferences and increased bar revenues by 46 percent. I have good problem-solving skills and am good with people. I am also well-organized, hard working, and detail-oriented. When may I come in for an interview?"

If you can't get an interview, it never hurts to ask for names of other people who might be able to help you. Add these new referrals to your network, and when you call them, remember to tell them who referred you.

E-mail Versus Phone Contact

E-mail offers a variety of advantages that a phone cannot. It's fast, free, and more convenient. You can attach files to it, such as resumes or JIST Cards, and can forward it to several people at once. Not to mention some employers prefer e-mail because they can deal with it on their own schedule.

E-mail has drawbacks, however. It is easily dismissed or deleted, and e-mails with attachments are viewed with suspicion nowadays. Phone calls, on the other hand, let you interact with employers in a more natural way and provide a more personal touch. Not to mention it is much harder for employers to say no to you on the phone when you are requesting an interview.

With all that in mind, you're better off using a combination of the two: e-mailing to reach more people faster and phone calls when you really want to make a connection and land an interview.